EARTH
SCIENCE
PROJECTS
★ for kids ★

A PROJECT GUIDE TO
THE
SOLAR
SYSTEM

Colleen Kessler

Mitchell Lane

P.O. Box 196
Hockessin, Delaware 19707
Visit us on the web: www.mitchelllane.com
Comments? email us: mitchelllane@mitchelllane.com

Mitchell Lane

EARTH SCIENCE PROJECTS for kids

A Project Guide to:
Earthquakes • Earth's Waters
Rocks and Minerals • **The Solar System**
Volcanoes • Wind, Weather, and the Atmosphere

**Library of Congress
Cataloging-in-Publication Data**

Kessler, Colleen.
  A project guide to the solar system / Colleen D. Kessler.
     p. cm. — (Earth science projects for kids)
  Includes bibliographical references and index.
  ISBN 978-1-58415-867-7 (lib. bd.)
  1. Solar system—Experiments—Juvenile literature. 2. Science projects—Juvenile literature. I. Title.

  QB501.3.K54 2011
  523.2078—dc22

                                        2010030946

Printing   1   2   3   4   5   6   7   8   9

                                        PLB

CONTENTS

Ptolemy

INTRODUCTION

The cosmos has fascinated observers since ancient times. People from Egypt, Greece, China, and other places around the world recorded their observations of the heavens. They noted that the bright white lights in the sky seemed to twinkle but did not move in relation to one another. People used the patterns of these lights (constellations) and the positions of them in the sky to know where to travel and to mark the seasons.

They also noticed that there were five lights that did not twinkle. These wandered across the sky every night—the Greeks called them planets (wanderers). On most nights the planets seemed to move from east to west, but they showed up in different parts of the sky each night. Sometimes they would travel quickly or slowly—and sometimes they stopped and went the other way! Ancient people thought that these odd movements seemed purposeful. They believed that these lights were gods moving through the heavens. It wasn't until the second century CE that a Greek astronomer named Ptolemy came up with an explanation for these movements that did not involve gods.

According to Ptolemy, Earth is a sphere. It never spins or moves. He theorized that Earth is the center of the cosmos and that all of the other planets and the Sun orbit it in circular paths. While we now know that this theory is wrong, it was widely accepted for more than a thousand years. It took a Polish mathematician and clergyman, Nicolaus Copernicus, to take the next step toward modern astronomy.

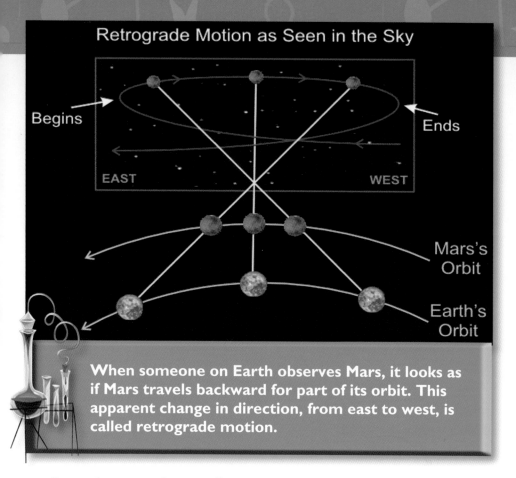

Retrograde Motion as Seen in the Sky

Begins

Ends

EAST

WEST

Mars's Orbit

Earth's Orbit

When someone on Earth observes Mars, it looks as if Mars travels backward for part of its orbit. This apparent change in direction, from east to west, is called retrograde motion.

Copernicus noted many flaws in Ptolemy's theories but could not voice them. The Catholic Church endorsed Ptolemy's views because it wanted people to believe that Earth was the most important part of the heavens. The Church threatened or imprisoned any person who went against this geocentric (or Earth-centered) view of the solar system.

Copernicus studied and wrote about his theories in silence. Just before his death, he published *On Revolutions of Heavenly Spheres*. This book detailed a heliocentric (or Sun-centered) solar system.

Despite the provable mathematics and evidence presented in Copernicus's theory, there were still flaws. Astronomers found that his theory could not predict the paths of the planets well. This was a puzzle that Johannes Kepler of Germany would solve with his laws of planetary motion. Kepler studied the observations Tycho Brahe made in an observatory in Prague (in what is now the Czech Republic). For years he

Johannes Kepler

looked over the observations Brahe had made of Mars. He tried different circular paths that would make sense. He finally realized that the orbit was elliptical, not circular.

This discovery explained many of the mysteries that had confused astronomers for centuries. It showed that planets were closer to the Sun at some points in their orbits, and when they were, they sped up. Though these observations became known as Kepler's laws, it took another astronomer and a special instrument to prove them to the world.

Galileo Galilei was an Italian scientist who heard about the invention of an instrument that could show faraway things as if they were close by. He built one that magnified to twenty times an object's size and used it to study the night sky. His improved telescope revolutionized modern astronomy. Using it, Galileo was able to prove that the planets orbited the Sun in elliptical paths, that each spun around its own axis, that the Moon was rough and pocked, and that Jupiter had four moons of its own.

Another remarkable scientist, Isaac Newton, observed the universal force that pulled on all objects—gravity. His description of the force and the laws he developed to define it were instrumental in explaining why objects behave the way they do. He realized that the larger the mass of an object, the larger its gravitational force. He also discovered that the farther one object is from another, the weaker the gravitational force is between them.

Newton also contributed by inventing a better telescope. While the instrument Galileo used was effective, it had problems. The edges of its lenses acted as prisms. This created halos of light around objects. Newton built the first reflecting telescope to get rid of these halos. While it was only 6 inches (15 centimeters) long, it was powerful enough to see detail on Jupiter's moons.

At first, astronomers used these telescopes to study the things they already knew about. Eventually, though, telescopes became more and more powerful. Scientists began to search the solar system and beyond. They made exciting discovery after exciting discovery. In 1781, German composer and astronomer William Herschel discovered Uranus. His discovery, and the strange behaviors of Uranus, led other scientists to believe that there might be an eighth planet. They believed that the gravitational force of this planet was acting on Uranus. After mathematicians sent him careful calculations, astronomer Johann Galle discovered Neptune in 1846.

Finally we had what we thought was a clear view of our solar system. It included the Sun and nine planets that orbit it: Mercury, Venus, Earth, Mars, Jupiter, Saturn, Uranus, Neptune, and Pluto. It also included the moons of these planets, asteroids, comets, dust, and other space debris influenced by the Sun. As scientists continued to revise their ideas about the solar system, they had second thoughts about calling Pluto a planet.

Like other sciences, the field of astronomy is constantly evolving. New discoveries and adaptations to old theories continue to be made. And, while the only celestial body we have touched is the Moon, we have been able to uncover many truths about space. We know that the outer planets are gas giants, and the inner planets are made up of rocky, terrestrial materials.

The dwarf planet classification is perhaps one of the greatest contributions to modern astronomy. In 2005, astronomer Mike Brown announced that a tenth planet had been discovered. Eris was ice-covered, bigger than Pluto, and like Pluto, orbited within the Kuiper Belt—a disk-shaped region of small, icy bodies. This discovery, instead of causing celebration, sparked debate. Astronomers had always considered Pluto the odd man out in our planetary system. It had never fit in with the terrestrial planets or the gas giants, and it was unable to force objects out of its path like the other planets can. When Pluto was discovered in 1930, nobody knew about Kuiper Belt objects—the billions of ice and rock chunks that orbit the Sun out

Pluto (left) and Eris

past Neptune. If Pluto and Eris were considered planets, should other huge asteroids and Kuiper Belt objects also be considered planets?

The International Astronomical Union settled the debate in 2006. They decided, after much controversy, that an object has to have three characteristics to be considered a planet. It must orbit the Sun, be large enough that its gravitational force pulls it into a sphere, and be able to clear smaller objects out of its orbit. A dwarf planet must have only the first two characteristics. Pluto was reclassified as a dwarf planet, leaving the solar system with only eight true planets.

More discoveries are being made as scientists continue to send missions into space. Scientists had thought the surface of the Moon was bone dry. On November 13, 2009, NASA announced that they had discovered water on the Moon. This exciting discovery might allow scientists to build a lunar space station. By continuing to ask questions, design missions, and test theories, they are proving previous theories false.

Activities and experiments like the ones in this book can also spark new insights into certain fields of science. They can broaden your mind. As you try these projects, please remember the following:

- **NEVER LOOK DIRECTLY AT THE SUN.** Even if the light seems dim to you, the powerful rays can permanently damage your eyes.
- You may be asked to work with a parent or other adult for some of the activities. Please do so.
- Most of the materials that you need for these activities can be found at home or at school. In some cases, you may need to purchase items from a teacher supply store or an online science store. These resources are listed on page 45.
- Keep track of all your experiments, thoughts, and discoveries in a science notebook. As you progress, you can flip back through your notes and maybe discover something new.

As you learn about science, it is important not to get caught up in the way things have always been described or thought of. New evidence and discoveries will emerge, changing how people view the universe. It is important to keep an open mind and have fun as you discover your world.

A display of planetary
images taken by spacecraft managed
by the Jet Propulsion Laboratory in
Pasadena, California. Included are
images of (from top to bottom) Mercury,
Venus, Earth (and Moon), Mars, Jupiter,
Saturn, Uranus, and Neptune.

BUILD A TELESCOPE

Galileo Galilei (1564–1642) is considered the first modern scientist because, through the use of telescopes, he proved that careful observation leads to more accurate understanding. With his telescopes and observation methods, scientists have been able to disprove much of ancient scientific thought. By experimenting, observing, and using tools to study the solar system, he and the scientists who followed realized that much of past theories were based on opinion, not fact.

One of his greatest contributions was the discovery of what are now called Galilean satellites. These are Jupiter's four largest moons: Io, Europa, Callisto, and Ganymede. He observed that Venus went through phases, indicating that it orbited the Sun, not Earth. These and other discoveries supported Copernicus's theories but violated church law.

Galileo was arrested by the Roman Catholic Church following the publication of his book, *Dialogue Concerning the Two Chief World Systems.* (The two systems were those of Ptolemy and Copernicus.) He was found guilty of heresy and was sentenced to spend the rest of his life under house arrest. However, he continued to write about his scientific observations.

Troubleshooting: If you can't bring your object into focus, try using a longer piece of card stock for your eyepiece tube, or a longer cardboard tube, such as a wrapping paper roll.

Try building a simple telescope just like Galileo did. You can order convex lenses from an online scientific supply store, or find them at a teacher supply store. They are inexpensive, usually only a few dollars each.

PROCEDURE
1. Roll a piece of card stock into a tube the approximate diameter of the smaller lens. This will be the eyepiece of the telescope.
2. Tape the eyepiece lens to one end of the card-stock tube as securely as you can.
3. Tape the second lens securely to the end of the paper towel tube.
4. Slide the empty end of the card-stock tube into the empty end of the paper towel tube.
5. Look through the eyepiece of your new telescope toward a distant object. Slide the tubes in and out until the object is in focus. The object should be magnified and upside down.

SATELLITE WALK

Space is full of interesting things to look for: comets, moons, planets, asteroids, and more. You can see any number of these things among the stars on given days if you just know where to look. But what about all of the satellites, debris, and space junk put up there by humans? That can all be seen, too. In fact, in 2010, the International Space Station was one of the biggest things visible in the night sky. Viewed from Earth, it can be as bright as the planet Venus and move as fast as a speeding jet.

On a clear night, you can try to spot some of the satellites and spacecraft orbiting Earth. Check out websites like http://heavens-above.com or http://spaceflight.nasa.gov/realdata/sightings. They list resources you can search to find out when the International Space Station, the Space Shuttle, or other objects will be visible from your backyard. You can use the telescope you made in the first experiment to help you find them.

PROCEDURE

1. On a clear, dark night, stand outside facing south, toward the equator.
2. Look for bright and steady points of white light moving quickly across the sky. Remember, blinking lights or red lights are not from satellites, they are from passing airplanes.
3. Most satellites will appear near the horizon to your right and speed quickly across the sky, disappearing to the left.
4. To see satellites that orbit the North Pole, find the North Star and search for passing white lights.

CHECK OUT THE MOON

One of the easiest celestial bodies to observe is the Moon. If you built the telescope in the first activity, you can use it to look at the sky and check out the Moon's surface. Otherwise, your eyes can do the job unaided.

Even though the Moon doesn't produce its own light, it is the brightest object in the sky. The Moon is Earth's only natural satellite. Beautiful as seen from our planet, the Moon is a bleak place. It is interesting to study despite its dreariness. Its surface is pocked and cratered from the impacts of meteoroids and asteroids.

In this activity you will become an expert on the Moon's behavior. What does it do each night? Does its position in the sky change? How long does it take for the Moon to go through its phases? Make sure you, like Galileo, make careful observations. Record what you see.

MATERIALS

* Notebook or paper
* Pen or pencil
* Weather section of daily newspaper with Moon information
* Duct tape or other marker
* Telescope from page 10
* Compass (optional)

The Moon and the Sun

PROCEDURE

1. Check out the weather section of your local paper to find out when the next full moon will appear.
2. Starting that night, go out and look for the Moon at sunset.
3. When you find it, use duct tape or some other marker to record your observation area.
4. Draw what the Moon looks like as the Sun sets.
5. Note where it is in the sky—use a compass if you wish.
6. Answer the following questions in your notebook:

   Which side of the Moon is brighter?

   Are there any distinguishing patterns anywhere on the Moon?
7. If the Sun and Moon are out at the same time, measure the distance between them. (**DO NOT LOOK DIRECTLY AT THE SUN!**) You can measure the approximate distance from the Sun to the Moon with your fists. Hold your closed fist straight out from your body toward the horizon. Make a fist with your other hand and extend your arm so that your fist sits on top of your other fist. Your fist represents a 10-degree angle. Continue going upward, fist over fist, until your arm is pointing straight up. It should take about 9 fist-over-fists to make this 90-degree angle. Scientists use angles like this to measure approximate distances between celestial bodies.
8. To find the distance between two celestial objects, like a planet and the Moon, cover one of them with your extended fist. Then, find out how many fists separate the two bodies. Multiply that number by 10, and you get the angle in degrees.
9. Observe what happens to the Moon after the Sun sets. What path does it take?
10. Observe the Moon from the same location, making the same observations and measurements, for the next two weeks. Do you notice any changes in the Moon's appearance or behavior? What do you see? Why do you think these changes occur? Record all of these observations in your notebook.

OBSERVING LUNAR ECLIPSES

The Moon passes through Earth's shadow to cause a lunar eclipse a few times each year. There are three types of lunar eclipses. A penumbral eclipse is when the Moon passes through Earth's penumbral shadow (see the diagram on page 20). These are tough to see. A partial eclipse occurs when part of the Moon passes through Earth's umbral shadow. Partial eclipses can be easily seen from Earth. The most interesting, though, are total eclipses. These occur when the entire Moon passes through Earth's umbral shadow.

During a total eclipse, Earth blocks the Sun's light, but the Moon is not in total darkness. As sunlight passes through Earth's atmosphere, it is filtered and bent. The atmosphere removes the blue light from the sunlight, giving the Moon an indirect reddish glow. Try viewing the next lunar eclipse scheduled for your area. NASA and others have posted eclipse schedules on the Internet.

PROCEDURE

1. If you are lucky enough to live where a lunar eclipse will be visible soon, go outside to a dark, clear area just before the eclipse is

MATERIALS

* Binoculars or telescope
* Internet access to find when and where the next lunar eclipse will happen, or to find a video of a lunar eclipse
* Notebook
* Pen or pencil
* Compass
* Camera (optional)

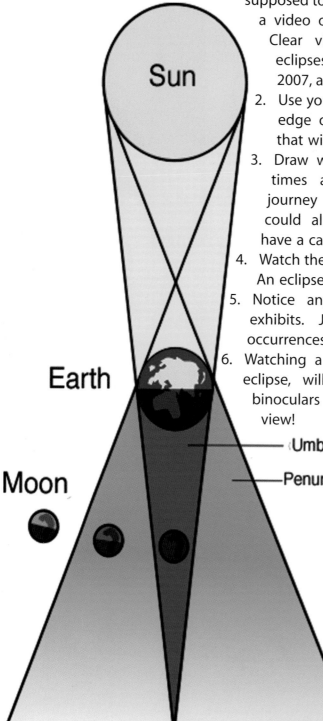

Sun

Earth

Moon

—— Umbra

——Penumbra

LEFT: The Moon passes through the penumbra, then glows red in the umbra.

supposed to happen. (If not, you can watch a video of an eclipse on the Internet. Clear videos are available for the eclipses that occurred on March 3, 2007, and February 20, 2008.)

2. Use your compass to find the eastern edge of the Moon. This is the side that will begin to darken first.

3. Draw what you see a few separate times as the Moon continues its journey through Earth's shadow. You could also take photographs if you have a camera.

4. Watch the eclipse for as long as you can. An eclipse can last nearly four hours.

5. Notice any color displays the moon exhibits. Jot down notes of these occurrences in your notebook.

6. Watching a lunar eclipse, unlike a solar eclipse, will not hurt your eyes. Use binoculars or a telescope to get a better view!

RIGHT: A series of images shows the Moon during a full lunar eclipse.

COCOA CRATERS

Impact craters are the impressions made by collisions of meteors and asteroids on the surface of planets and moons. The Moon is covered with impact craters. It has no atmosphere to protect it from these impacts, so it is constantly bombarded. Earth's atmosphere burns up most objects so that they are either gone or microscopic by the time they reach the surface. Craters have different shapes and sizes, depending on the shape, size, and speed of the object that slammed into it. In this activity, you can try to discover how different-shaped craters form by dropping objects onto your own "lunar surface."

PROCEDURE

1. Spread old newspaper all over your work surface (table, floor, deck, etc.).
2. Mix the flour and the salt together in the pan.
3. Use the spatula to smooth out this "lunar surface."
4. Sprinkle the cocoa powder across the surface of the "moon" to help your craters show up better.

MATERIALS

* Old newspaper
* 2 cups of flour
* 2 cups of salt
* Metal baking pan
* Spatula
* 5 to 6 tablespoons of cocoa powder
* Small stones, marbles, shells, or coins to serve as asteroids and meteoroids

5. Hold one of your meteoroids about a foot from the pan and drop it onto the lunar surface.
6. Drop three or four meteoroids in the same way.
7. Compare your impact craters. How are they the same? Different? Which is the deepest? The widest?

UNEARTHING MICROMETEORITES

A comet is a dirty snowball of ice and rock that orbits the Sun in a long, elliptical path. A common misconception is that comets have long, flowing tails at all times. In reality, comets do have long tails. These tails appear as they near the Sun. The heat from the Sun warms them and melts their ice. The stream of melting gases creates a coma (head). The reflection of sunlight off this cloud of melting gas is what we can see from Earth. Solar winds blow the cloud away from the Sun, and we see a tail-like trail following the nucleus.

Most meteoroids come from asteroids and comets that have been broken apart by collisions in space. They are small and travel at varying speeds. Meteoroids can be made of rock, metals, and ice. Most people think of streaks of light in the sky when they think of meteoroids. The streak, called a meteor, is the result of a meteoroid that entered the Earth's atmosphere and burned up. When a meteoroid reaches Earth's surface, it is called a meteorite. These specimens from space are great samples for scientists to study. They contain some of the same materials that formed the solar system billions of years ago and can give scientists information about the origin of the planets.

MATERIALS

* 2 small glass dishes, one filled with rainwater and one with distilled water
* Strong magnet
* Plastic bag
* Hot plate or stovetop
* Needle
* Oven mitt
* Tongs
* **An adult**
* Microscope with slides

Earth is constantly bombarded by objects and dust from space. Tons of metallic and rocky micrometeorites fall to Earth every day. It is possible to find and study these. Once you have followed the directions for collecting your micrometeorites, look at them carefully through a microscope. You are looking for round, pitted bits of metal. These particles may be as old as the solar system itself—4.6 billion years!

PROCEDURE

1. Place a magnet inside a plastic bag.
2. Drag it through the dish of rainwater.
3. Place the bag into the dish of distilled water, remove the magnet, and shake the bag so that any particles fall into the distilled water.
4. **Under adult supervision,** heat the dish on a hot plate or stove until the water has evaporated. Let the dish cool.
5. Stroke the needle with the magnet, starting at the eye and ending at the point. Do this 50 to 100 times, always in the same direction.
6. Drag the magnetized needle along the bottom and sides of the dish. Tap the needle onto a microscope slide.
7. Observe the sediment under the microscope.

SUNSET TRACKING

The Sun rises in the east and sets in the west every day. It is the driving force of our solar system. The Sun's gravitational pull holds everything in its place. Without the energy we receive from the Sun, Earth as we know it would not exist. The nuclear reactions within its layers heat our planet. It provides plants with the energy they need for photosynthesis. It keeps our temperature in a range that supports life.

Scientists observe the behaviors of celestial bodies like the Sun to learn more about how the cosmos works. In this activity you will observe the setting sun for a month. Make sure you make and record observations carefully. Pay special attention to any patterns you notice. Remember: **NEVER LOOK DIRECTLY AT THE SUN!**

PROCEDURE

1. Find a spot in your yard that offers an unobstructed view of the sunset. Mark the spot with duct tape.
2. Visit the spot at sunset, drawing what you see in your notebook.
3. Use your compass to mark the cardinal directions (North, South, East, West) on your drawing.

MATERIALS
* Notebook or paper
* Pen or pencil
* Compass
* Duct tape

4. Using your fist in the same fist-over-fist method you used in Check Out the Moon (see page 17), record the Sun's altitude.
5. Twice a week for the next month, go back to your marked spot and draw another picture, labeling the directions, date, and time.
6. After a month, look back at your drawings and notes. Does the Sun's setting location change throughout the month?

MAKE A
SUNDIAL

As far back as 5000 BCE, people used the Sun to estimate time. Sundials may have started as simple sticks in the ground. Each stick would cast a shadow on the ground, and as the shadow moved, people could track the passage of time. Ancient Egyptians and Babylonians built obelisks. The shadows of these four-sided monuments divided the day between "before noon" and "after noon." Eventually, more accurate sundials were built.

People discovered that a shadow cast by a slanted object was an accurate timekeeper. The slanted object, called a gnomon, casts a shadow on the face of the sundial. Sundials have faces that are divided into twelve sections. The Sun moves across the sky and casts a shadow. This shades one of the divided sections and tells the time.

You can build a simple sundial, too. The most important thing to remember before you begin this activity is to position your sundial in the place you want it to stay. If you move it around, the sections you mark for the time will no longer be accurate.

MATERIALS

* Large piece of poster board
* Block of wood or wooden dowel, about an inch (2 centimeters) in diameter
* Hot glue gun
* Permanent marker
* **An adult**

Ptolemy stone, Annapolis, Maryland. Greek astronomer Ptolemy invented the stone to measure the altitude of the Sun.

PROCEDURE

1. With the help of **an adult,** use the glue gun to hot-glue your wooden block or dowel to the center of a sheet of poster board. This is your gnomon.
2. Take your sundial out to a sunny spot in your yard where it will not be disturbed.
3. Every hour, go out into the yard and mark the shadow with your permanent marker to show the time of day.
4. As long as you leave your sundial in place, you will have an accurate measure of the time of day!

UNROLL THE SOLAR SYSTEM

The distance between objects in the universe is immense, even in our "crowded" solar system. When scientists talk about these distances, they use terms like *astronomical unit* (the distance from Earth to the Sun—93 million miles, or 150 million kilometers) and *light-year* (the distance light travels through a vacuum in one year—about 5.88 trillion miles, or 9.46 trillion kilometers). These terms are helpful, but they are so immense, it is still hard to understand the true scale of our solar system. In this activity, you will create a pocket-sized model of the solar system. Amaze your friends as you "unroll" the planets at their feet!

MATERIALS
* Brand-new roll of cash register tape, at least 150 feet long (available at office supply stores)
* Colored pencils
* Tape measure
* Chart on page 31
* Photos of objects on chart (optional)
* Glue (optional)

Celestial Object	Average Distance from Sun in miles	Average Distance from Sun in astronomical units (AU)	Approximate Distance from the Previous Object on Tape
Sun	–	–	–
Mercury	36 million	0.4	14 inches
Venus	67 million	0.7	12 inches
Earth	93 million	1.0	10 inches
Moon	93 million	1.0	0.1 inch
Mars	142 million	1.5	19 inches
Asteroid/Kuiper Belt	256 million	2.7	3 feet 8 inches
Jupiter	483 million	5.2	7 feet 4 inches
Saturn	885 million	9.5	13 feet
Uranus	1,787 million	19.2	29 feet
Neptune	2,800 million	30	32 feet 8 inches
Pluto	3,699 million	39.7	29 feet
Oort Cloud	11,700,000 million	122,580	about 70 miles

PROCEDURE

1. The scale that you will use to reconstruct the solar system on your cash register tape is 93 million miles (1 astronomical unit) = 3 feet. Use the chart to space your planets.
2. Start by drawing the Sun at the tip of the cash register tape.
3. Then, according to the chart, draw Mercury 14 inches from the Sun.
4. Next, draw Venus 12 inches from Mercury.
5. Continue drawing the solar system by referencing the table above. You will be able to use your cash register tape to draw as far out as the dwarf planet Pluto. Notice on the table that the next closest thing in the solar system, the Oort Cloud, would be about 70 miles from your drawn Pluto—imagine the length of that tape!
6. If you want to add interest to your solar system roll, print pictures of the celestial bodies you marked, and glue them to your tape.

Tycho Brahe

PLANETARY ORBITAL PATHS

Johannes Kepler (1571–1630) became a champion of Copernicus's theory of a heliocentric solar system when he was in college. As an adult he became an assistant to Tycho Brahe (1546–1601), a Danish astronomer who is credited with the most accurate observations of the solar system up until that time. Kepler used Brahe's data to figure out that the planets move in elliptical, not circular, orbits around the Sun. He also realized that the planets speed up when their orbits bring them closer to the Sun and slow down the farther from the Sun they travel. Using the materials in this activity, create a drawing of a planet's elliptical orbit.

PROCEDURE

1. Tape a piece of cardboard to a flat surface.
2. Measure the halfway point on each horizontal edge and connect the two by drawing a straight line across the cardboard with your pencil.

* A piece of cardboard
* Pencil
* Two pushpins
* Masking tape
* 6-inch string tied tightly into a loop
* Ruler

Sun

3. Measure the halfway point on each vertical edge and connect the two by drawing a straight line with your pencil. You should now have two lines that intersect at the center of the cardboard.
4. Push one of the pins into the point on the cardboard where the lines intersect. This represents the Sun.
5. Put the other pushpin about 3 inches (7.5 centimeters) from the first pin, along the horizontal line that you drew.
6. Loop the string so that it goes around both pushpins.
7. Hold your pencil upright, inside the string, and stretch it until it is taut.
8. Draw an "orbit" around the "Sun." Your orbit will be an elliptical path around the Sun. Notice how the pencil is farther away from the Sun at some points on its orbital path.

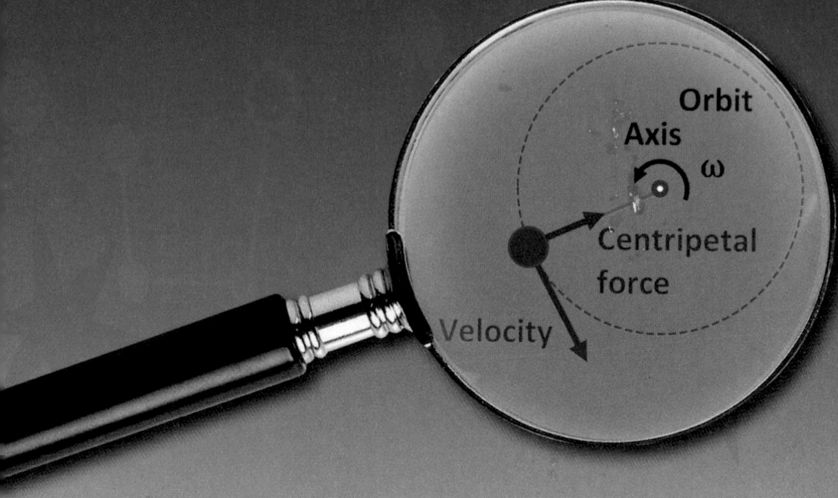

The diagram shows a magnifying glass focused on an orbit with labels: **Orbit**, **Axis**, ω, **Centripetal force**, and **Velocity**.

CENTRIPETAL FORCE

Isaac Newton (1642–1727) developed three laws of motion:

1) Every object that is in uniform motion will remain in motion unless an outside force acts upon it.
2) The force (F) on an object is determined by the product of the object's mass (m) and acceleration (a): $F = ma$.
3) Every action has an equal and opposite reaction.

He theorized that his laws would work in space as well as on Earth.

When Newton observed that the planets moved in regular orbits, he recognized that some force was acting on them. This force kept them from moving off in a straight line. He believed that it was the gravitational force of the Sun acting on the planets from a distance. Modern scientists agree with his theory.

Any force that causes objects to move in a curved path is called centripetal force. Centripetal force from the Sun's gravitational pull acts on all objects in the solar system. You can experience the power of centripetal force with a bucket, rope, and water.

MATERIALS
* ✱ Small bucket
* ✱ 2-foot-long rope
* ✱ Water
* ✱ Large open space, outside

PROCEDURE

1. Tie one end of the rope securely to the bucket handle.
2. Fill the bucket halfway with water.
3. Go outside to a large open space.
4. Hold the other end of the rope in one hand.
5. Spin the bucket in a very fast circle. What is happening?
6. What would happen if you let go of the rope? Why? (Do not try this unless you are in a wide-open outdoor space.)

If the rope breaks or you let it go, the bucket will fly off in a straight line. This tells you that a force was pulling the bucket toward you, keeping it from flying off. Your hold was acting like the Sun's gravity on a planet.

BUILD A SPECTROSCOPE

Scientists have found that light can act like particles or waves. The amount of energy in light can be classified by the light's wavelength. (A wavelength is the distance between two waves; see the diagram above.) Different wavelengths of light appear as different colors. Different elements emit different wavelengths of light, so they have their own patterns of color.

Scientists realized that they could split the light from objects and celestial bodies into the wavelengths that make it up. They could use this light to learn more about the elements that objects are made of. A spectroscope is the tool that helps them do this. It spreads out the colors of an object's light into bright lines.

Scientists also use spectroscopes to measure the speed of objects in space. Called the Doppler effect, wavelengths are shorter when objects are moving toward the viewer; they are longer as they move away from the viewer.

Once you've built the spectroscope in this project, you'll be able to hold it under the different lights in your home. It will reveal the components of those lights.

MATERIALS

* Scissors
* Heavy dark-colored card stock
* Ruler
* Plastic coffee can lid
* Heavy tape, such as electrical tape
* Old CD (one that is not needed anymore)
* Craft knife (have **an adult** help you with this tool)
* Bright light

PROCEDURE

1. Use scossors to cut a 1¼-inch-high and ¼-inch-wide slit in the middle of one of the long sides of your card stock (see the photograph above).
2. Roll the card stock into a tube, and set the un-notched side into the plastic lid, making sure it fits securely. Do not tape the lid in place yet.
3. Tape the tube securely.
4. With the notched side up, place the CD shiny-side down on top of the tube and tape it in place, making sure your notch stays rectangular.
5. With **an adult's help,** use a craft knife to cut a very thin 2-inch-long slit in the plastic lid.
6. Cover the tube with the lid, making the slit perpendicular to the notch.
7. Place the spectroscope directly under a bright light so that light enters through the slit in the plastic lid.

German lensmaker Joseph von Fraunhofer demonstrates the spectroscope around 1820. He discovered that light from the planets, Moon, and Sun have the same pattern, but light from other bright stars have unique patterns.

8. Look through the notch while you shine the light through the slit.

9. Tilt the spectroscope back and forth until you see a rainbow on the CD. If you can't see a rainbow, your slit may be too big or too small. If you think it's too big, use electrical tape to make it smaller. If you think it's too small, have **an adult** help you enlarge it.

10. Once you are able to see the rainbow, your spectroscope is done! You can now use it to check the spectra of different types of lights to see how the rainbow pattern changes in different light. Hold it under lamps and outside in the sunlight—but **DO NOT LOOK DIRECTLY AT THE SUN!**

While most of the lights you observe will have different color patterns because they emit different wavelengths of light, you may find some that emit the same pattern of light waves.

39

THE BULK OF BEING IN SPACE

When astronauts travel to space, they have jobs to do. Whatever their mission, they need to figure out ways to work in challenging situations. There is no air for them to breathe. The temperatures are extreme. They must wear loads of protective gear while completing highly specialized tasks. To get a feel for what it is like to work in space, try this activity. You just might not take simple tasks for granted anymore!

PROCEDURE
1. Put on the coat and fasten it tightly.
2. Stuff the space between the coat and your body with crumpled newspapers until it is difficult to move. (You may need someone to help you with this.)
3. Pull on the gloves that fit.
4. Put on the oversize gloves.
5. Try to do small tasks: pick up coins and put them inside a piggy bank, put together a puzzle, put a nut and bolt together, etc.

MATERIALS
* An adult's winter coat
* Old newspaper
* Gloves that fit your hand
* Oversize adult gloves
* Tasks that have small pieces, such as puzzles, coins and a piggy bank, nuts and bolts

BUILD A ROCKET

Rockets had been around for hundreds of years before scientists began thinking about how they could use them to explore space. Many scientists contributed to the science of studying rockets and the idea of using them for space travel. Each scientist built upon the ideas of earlier scientists. That is really the key to rocket science—testing different designs and learning from mistakes.

Newton's third law of motion explains rocket propulsion. This law states that for every action there is an equal and opposite reaction. Rocket engineers use this law by creating a high-pressure gas inside the rocket that can escape in only one direction. When the gas comes bursting out of the rocket's base, it pushes the rocket in the opposite direction: up.

As you test the rocket you build in this activity, pay attention to how it behaves. Are there improvements you could make to get it to fly higher? Straighter? Treat this experiment like any good scientist would: Observe carefully, and write down your results. Don't forget to wear safety goggles.

MATERIALS

* Water
* Small plastic container with a snap-on lid, such as a 35 mm film canister
* Effervescent antacid tablets such as Alka-Seltzer tablets
* 8½-by-11-inch construction paper
* Card stock
* Masking or packaging tape
* Marker
* Scissors
* Safety goggles

PROCEDURE

1. Line up the open end of a plastic container with the short edge of a sheet of paper.
2. Tape the long side of the paper to the container, leaving about ½ inch of the container exposed so that the lid will fit securely when replaced.
3. Roll the paper around the container to form the tubular body of your rocket. Secure it with tape.
4. Cut out four fins and a nose from the card stock. Tape them to your rocket.
5. Take your rocket, lid, water, and antacid tablets outside to a wide open space.
6. Put on safety goggles.
7. Pour water into the container until it is about half full.
8. Drop in an antacid tablet and QUICKLY snap the lid in place, set your rocket down, and step back.

Books

Aguilar, David. *11 Planets: A New View of the Solar System.* New York: National Geographic Children's Books, 2008.

Benson, Michael. *Beyond a Solar System Voyage.* New York: Abrams Books for Young Readers, 2009.

Dickinson, Terrence. *NightWatch: A Practical Guide to Viewing the Universe.* New York: Firefly Books, 2006.

Scott, Elaine. *When Is a Planet Not a Planet? The Story of Pluto.* New York: Clarion Books, 2007.

Simon, Seymour. *Our Solar System* (revised edition). New York: HarperCollins, 2007.

Works Consulted

Axelrod, Alan, PhD, and Christopher DePree, PhD. *The Complete Idiot's Guide to Astronomy, 4th Edition.* Indianapolis: Alpha, 2008.

Bruning, David. "Astronomy in the Classroom: Building Astronomy's Future." *Astronomy,* September 1993: 40.

Chaisson, Eric, and Steve McMillan. *Astronomy: A Beginner's Guide to the Universe, 5th Edition.* San Francisco: Benjamin Cummings, 2006.

Chang, Kenneth. "NASA Finds 'Significant' Water on Moon—CNN.com." *CNN. com—Breaking News, U.S., World, Weather, Entertainment & Video News.* November 13, 2009. http://www.cnn.com/2009/TECH/space/11/13/water. moon.nasa/index.html

Gingerich, Owen. *The Book Nobody Read: Chasing the Revolutions of Nicolaus Copernicus.* Boston: Walker & Company, 2004.

NASA: *Solar System Exploration.* June 2, 2009. http://solarsystem.nasa.gov/index.cfm

Thompson, Andrea. "SPACE.com—It's Official: Water Found on the Moon." *Space.com,* September 23, 2009. http://www.space.com/scienceastronomy/090923-moon-water-discovery.html

On the Internet

Amazing Space
    http://amazing-space.stsci.edu/
Astronomy for Kids
    http://www.kidsastronomy.com/solar_system.htm
Espenak, Fred. *Mr. Eclipse:* "Lunar Eclipses for Beginners."
    http://www.mreclipse.com/Special/LEprimer.html
NASA Science for Kids
    http://nasascience.nasa.gov/kids/kids-solar-system
NASA Solar System Exploration
    http://solarsystem.nasa.gov/kids/index.cfm

Science and Teacher Supply Companies

Science Kit Store
    http://sciencekitstore.com/
Science Kit & Boreal Laboratories
    http://sciencekit.com/Default.asp?bhcd2=1258230685
Steve Spangler Science Store
    http://www.stevespanglerscience.com/

altitude (AL-tih-tood)—Angular height above the horizon.

asteroid (AS-tuh-royd)—A small, rocky celestial body.

astronomer (uh-STRAH-nuh-mer)—A scientist who studies the planets, stars, and other objects in space.

atmosphere (AT-mus-feer)—The gases that surround a moon or planet.

celestial (seh-LES-chee-ul)—Relating to the sky or heavenly bodies.

centripetal force (sen-TRIH-pih-tul FORS)—The inward pull on a body as it orbits another body.

constellation (kon-stuh-LAY-shun)—A group of stars that form a pattern when viewed from Earth.

cosmos (KOZ-mohs)—The universe.

dwarf planet—A celestial body that orbits the Sun and has enough gravity to pull itself into a sphere.

eclipse (ee-KLIPS)—The passing of one celestial body through the shadow of another.

elliptical (ee-LIP-tih-kul)—Oval.

geocentric (jee-oh-SEN-trik)—Earth-centered.

gnomon (NOH-mun)—The part of a sundial that casts a shadow.

gravity (GRAH-vih-tee)—The force of attraction between all masses in the universe.

heliocentric (hee-lee-oh-SEN-trik)—Sun-centered.

International Astronomical Union (in-ter-NAH-shuh-nul as-troh-NAH-mih-kul YOON-yun)—A worldwide group of professional astronomers active in research and education in astronomy.

Kuiper Belt (KY-per BELT)—The disk-shaped region of small celestial bodies that orbit the Sun, including asteroids, comets, and dwarf planets, found past Neptune's orbit.

lunar (LOO-nur)—Of the Moon.

meteoroid (MEE-tee-uh-royd)—A small particle of dust or debris from space.

NASA—The National Aeronautics and Space Administration, the U.S. government agency responsible for space flight and aviation.

satellite (SAT-uh-lyt)—A natural or human-made object that orbits Earth or another celestial body.

spectroscope (SPEK-troh-skohp)—An instrument that splits light into its separate wavelengths (which can be seen as colors).

sundial (SUN-dy-ul)—A device that marks time when the Sun casts a shadow on its face or dial.

telescope (TEH-luh-skohp)—A tool that uses mirrors and lenses to magnify distant objects.

terrestrial (tuh-RES-tree-ul)—Having to do with Earth or being similar to Earth.

ABOUT THE AUTHOR

Colleen Kessler is the author of science books for kids, including *A Project Guide to Reptiles and Birds* and *A Project Guide to Sponges, Worms, and Mollusks* for Mitchell Lane Publishers. A former teacher of gifted students, Colleen now satisfies her curiosity as a full-time nonfiction writer. She does her researching and writing in her home office overlooking a wooded backyard in Northeastern Ohio. You can often find her blasting off rockets or searching for salamanders with her husband, Brian, and kids, Trevor, Molly, and Logan, or talking to schoolchildren about the excitement of studying science and nature. Find out more about Colleen at http://www.colleen-kessler.com.